14 Scriptural Principles for Daily Living Vol. 4

14
Scriptural Principles for Daily Living Vol. 4

"Your words are a flashlight to light the path ahead of me and keep me from stumbling."
[Psalm 119:105 TLB]

Anthony Adefarakan

GLOEM, CANADA

CONTENTS

Dedication	1
Acknowledgement	2
Introduction	4
Principle #1 — The Truth Is Not Bitter	7
Principle #2 — What Do You Believe?	11
Principle #3 — Recognizing Your Helpers	15

CONTENTS

Principle #4 | Staying Redeemed — 21

Principle #5 | Becoming a Worthy Representative — 25

Principle #6 | Escaping Spiritual Misery — 29

Principle #7 | Inexplicable Grace — 32

Principle #8 | Jesus' Love Language — 37

Principle #9 | Invest – Don't Spend — 42

Principle #10 | Stop Tolerating It — 45

Principle #11 | Nothing Can Separate You — 49

CONTENTS

Principle #12	Repent	52
Principle #13	He Has All The Answers	55
Principle #14	Walking in the Spirit	59
	Conclusion	62
	WHY YOU REALLY NEED JESUS!	63
	PRAYER POINTS	68
	BECOME A FINANCIAL PARTNER WITH JESUS	70
	About the Author	73
		76

Dedication

I dedicate this book to God Almighty for His goodness and faithfulness in making His Word available to me. All glory to His Holy Name.

Also to everyone desirous of a closer walk with God, living out His precepts on a daily basis, I am in agreement with you all and I decree that grace for a closer walk with God is coming upon you in Jesus' Name.

Acknowledgement

I sincerely acknowledge my Eternal Father, Who alone is the Source of all wisdom. He is the Author and Finisher of my faith and it is of His fullness that the contents of this book have been drawn.

Also, I want to profoundly appreciate my dear parents – Prince and Mrs. Timothy Adefarakan – for bringing me up in the way of the Lord and for instilling righteousness consciousness in me. The wonderful education foundation I was given, coupled with their constant encouragement has empowered me to reach heights that were once beyond my imagination.

My most special appreciation goes to my sweetheart, Abisolami; without her help and support, I would never have enjoyed the conducive atmosphere needed to publish this book. I appreciate your love, encouragement, and the support you give at all times. Thank you so much. I love you, my Baby!

And to all my mentors in Ministry, I appreciate you all. Your investments in my life are not in vain. May the Lord reward you all in Jesus' Name.

Introduction

Life on earth has been described as a form of pilgrimage with eternity as man's final destination.

1 Peter 2:11 TLB says:

"Dear brothers, you are only visitors here. Since your real home is in heaven, I beg you to keep away from the evil pleasures of this world; they are not for you, for they fight against your very souls."

And Hebrews 11:13 also says:

"These men of faith I have mentioned died without ever receiving all that God had promised them; but they saw it all awaiting them on ahead and were glad, for they agreed that this earth was not their real home but that they were just strangers visiting down here."

In the course of this brief earthly sojourn, we

are bound to face certain situations capable of generating questions like *'what step do I take?' 'where do I settle?' 'who do I marry?' 'will I be rich or poor?' 'how do I finance my projects?' 'how do I take good care of my family?' 'how do I know God's will for my life?'* just to mention a few. Usually, we find it difficult to provide correct answers to these questions due to our weak mortal nature.

However, there is a manual for this pilgrimage, which is the Word of God. The One Who designed this journey for us has put in the manual all we need to navigate our way successfully and to eventually end up on the glorious side of eternity when the pilgrimage is over. Little wonder David prayed in Psalm 119:19 – *"I am a stranger in the earth; hide not thy commandment from me".*

The principles presented in this Volume 4 are all Bible-based and will deliver results every time they are applied because the Word of God is forever settled in Heaven (Psalm 119:89).

I pray as you read on, God's grace to apply these principles will rest upon you in Jesus' Name.

Anthony Adefarakan.

Principle #1

The Truth Is Not Bitter

Psalm 119:103 KJV says *"How sweet are thy words unto my taste! yea, sweeter than honey to my mouth!"*

And Jeremiah 15:16 KJV says *"Thy words were found, and I did eat them; and thy word was unto me the joy and rejoicing of mine heart: for I am called by thy name, O LORD God of hosts."*

You may have heard people say "truth is bitter", well that's if you only had a bite. But if you really chew and eat the TRUTH, I tell you with all assurance, it is SWEET! Psalm 141:6 KJV says *'...they shall hear my words; for they are sweet.'*

The Word of God contains promises of fruitfulness to those who are barren; how could such truth be bitter?

The Word of God promises healing to those who are sick; how could such truth be bitter?

The Word of God promises wealth and prosperity to those who are in lack; how could such truth be bitter?

The Word of God is full of good promises, capable of turning anyone's bitter experiences into sweet ones.

Now, I get it, people use that expression (truth is bitter) to explain that the truth has to be told even though no one wants to hear it. I understand that part. But considering the truth the Word of God contains, it is sweet and therefore should attract excited attention.

The only time people should be afraid to hear the truth of the Word of God is if they are on the wrong side of the truth. For instance, the Word of God says *'the soul that sinneth shall die'*. So if you are a sinner, you are definitely on the wrong side of that truth, and to you, it may taste bitter. You see the way it works?

If on the other hand you are living a holy life and you read Proverbs 10:24 KJV which says *'the desire of the righteous shall be granted'*, you are definitely going to be happy because that tastes sweet. So you see it's not that the truth is really bitter (especially the truth the Word of God contains); it all depends on the side you are on. If the truth of the Word of God still tastes bitter to you, and you find it so difficult to accept, digest, or relate with, I strongly recommend you change your position. You must be on the right side (which is the Lord's side) before you can begin to experience the sweetness of the Word of God.

It is also worthy of note that even if you are on the right side, you may still sense or experience some bitterness when you attempt to 'eat' the Word. It usually happens when all you do is 'bite'. I will explain this to you. You see a particular scripture and you just 'bite' it (by only reading and interpreting it literally), it may taste bitter because there is no depth. However, if you take your time to really 'eat' (meditate on) that same scripture, you will discover how sweet it is. That's what happened to prophet Jeremiah in our second opening text. He 'ate' the Word and his heart rejoiced.

Principle #2

What Do You Believe?

James 2:19 NLT says *"You say you have faith, for you believe that there is one God. Good for you! Even the demons believe this, and they tremble in terror."*

As a believer, it is not enough to just believe in God. Our opening text suggests that just believing that there is one God puts you in the same category as demons.

To really be a believer, you must believe other things like the total counsel of God, His Word, His ways, His plans and purposes, His instructions,

His promises, His power, His love, His mercy, His grace, His judgments, His choices, etc.

For instance, as a believer, you should believe that you can do all things through Christ Who strengthens you according to Philippians 4:13 regardless of how you currently feel. You should also believe that regardless of what the economy of your country is saying, all things work together for your good according to Romans 8:28. In addition, you definitely should believe that no sinner will go unpunished according to Proverbs 11:21, and that should make you run from sin.

Going to church doesn't make you a believer, what makes you one is what you believe according to God's Word. Look at the encounter Mary had with Angel Gabriel in Luke 1:26-38 KJV;

"And in the sixth month the angel Gabriel was sent from God unto a city of Galilee, named Nazareth, To a virgin espoused to a man whose name was Joseph, of the house of David; and the virgin's name was Mary. And the angel came in unto

her, and said, Hail, thou that art highly favoured, the Lord is with thee: blessed art thou among women. And when she saw him, she was troubled at his saying, and cast in her mind what manner of salutation this should be. And the angel said unto her, Fear not, Mary: for thou hast found favour with God. And, behold, thou shalt conceive in thy womb, and bring forth a son, and shalt call his name JESUS. He shall be great, and shall be called the Son of the Highest: and the Lord God shall give unto him the throne of his father David: And he shall reign over the house of Jacob for ever; and of his kingdom there shall be no end.

Then said Mary unto the angel, How shall this be, seeing I know not a man? And the angel answered and said unto her, The Holy Ghost shall come upon thee, and the power of the Highest shall overshadow thee: therefore also that holy thing which shall be born of thee shall be called the Son of God. And, behold, thy cousin Elisabeth, she hath also conceived a son in her old age: and this is the sixth month with her, who was called barren. For with God nothing shall be impossible. And Mary said,

Behold the handmaid of the Lord; be it unto me according to thy word. And the angel departed from her".

Mary had no reason to believe the message Angel Gabriel brought to her. She was a virgin (she had never been involved in sexual intercourse), so how was she going to get pregnant without intercourse? Nevertheless, despite her situation which made becoming pregnant look unlikely, she chose to believe in God because all things are possible with Him. That's why she said in verse 38; '*...be it unto me according to your word.*' And because she believed when it didn't make any sense to believe, God fulfilled His promise to her and she became the Mother of our Lord Jesus Christ.

Are you a believer? Ask yourself: 'What do I believe?'

Principle #3

Recognizing Your Helpers

1 Samuel 30:1-20 KJV says *"And it came to pass, when David and his men were come to Ziklag on the third day, that the Amalekites had invaded the south, and Ziklag, and smitten Ziklag, and burned it with fire; And had taken the women captives, that were therein: they slew not any, either great or small, but carried them away, and went on their way. So David and his men came to the city, and, behold, it was burned with fire; and their wives, and their sons, and their daughters, were taken captives. Then David and the people that were with him lifted up their voice and wept, until they had no more power to weep. And David's two wives were taken captives, Ahinoam the Jezreelitess, and Abi-*

gail the wife of Nabal the Carmelite. And David was greatly distressed; for the people spake of stoning him, because the soul of all the people was grieved, every man for his sons and for his daughters: but David encouraged himself in the LORD his God.

And David said to Abiathar the priest, Ahimelech's son, I pray thee, bring me hither the ephod. And Abiathar brought thither the ephod to David. And David inquired at the LORD, saying, Shall I pursue after this troop? shall I overtake them? And he answered him, Pursue: for thou shalt surely overtake them, and without fail recover all. So David went, he and the six hundred men that were with him, and came to the brook Besor, where those that were left behind stayed. But David pursued, he and four hundred men: for two hundred abode behind, which were so faint that they could not go over the brook Besor.

And they found an Egyptian in the field, and brought him to David, and gave him bread, and he did eat; and they made him drink water; And they gave him a piece of a cake of figs, and two clusters of raisins: and when he had eaten, his spirit came again to him: for he had eaten no bread, nor drunk any water, three days and three nights. And David said unto him, To whom belongest thou? and whence art thou? And he said, I am a young man of Egypt, servant to an Amalekite; and my master left me, because three days agone I fell sick. We made an invasion upon the south of the Cherethites, and upon the coast which belongeth to Judah, and upon the south of Caleb; and we burned Ziklag with fire. And David said to him, Canst thou bring me down to this company? And he said, Swear unto me by God, that thou wilt neither kill me, nor deliver me into the hands of my master, and I will bring thee down to this company.

And when he had brought him down, behold, they were spread abroad upon all the earth, eating and drinking, and dancing, because of all the great spoil that they had taken out of the land of the Philistines, and out of the land of Judah. And David smote them from the twilight even unto the evening of the next day: and there escaped not a man of them, save four hundred young men, which rode upon camels, and fled. And David recovered all that the Amalekites had carried away: and David rescued his two wives. And there was nothing lacking to them, neither small nor great, neither sons nor daughters, neither spoil, nor any thing that they had taken to them: David recovered all. And David took all the flocks and the herds, which they drave before those other cattle, and said, This is David's spoil."

The Lord had assured David after he suffered a major loss that he would without fail recover all. He believed what the Lord had told him, so he stepped out in faith.

How did God direct him to where his recovery would take place? He deliberately positioned an Egyptian servant (who was sick and almost dying) on his way. Ordinarily, David would have nothing to do with such a fellow, but because he had the eyes of the spirit to recognize his helper, he fed him (the servant), and the moment he was revived, he took David and his men to where they recovered all they had lost. Recognizing your helper!

If they had killed that boy, it's possible they would have missed their opportunity for recovering their losses. Helpers of destiny do not always appear in suits or gorgeous attires. They may be dressed in rags but their inputs in your life can place you where you are destined to be. It took a prisoner to recommend Joseph to the top. Look down on no one! You will not miss your Helpers in Jesus' Name.

Also, take note of this, until you have helped someone, you may not be helped. So don't just pray for help, start helping others. And don't wait until all your needs are met before you start meeting the needs of others. As a matter of fact, one of the fastest ways to get your needs met is by becoming serious about meeting others' needs. May the grace to render help to those in need come upon you in Jesus' Name.

Remember this as well, it is not yet helping until the recipient sees it as such. Meeting needs is not necessarily a function of what you are willing to give but what the one in need requires. Giving $100 in time of urgent need may worth a whole lot more to someone than offering them $10,000 at a time when it is not needed. Render help with UNDERSTANDING!

Principle #4

Staying Redeemed

Galatians 5:16-24 KJV says *"This I say then, Walk in the Spirit, and ye shall not fulfil the lust of the flesh. For the flesh lusteth against the Spirit, and the Spirit against the flesh: and these are contrary the one to the other: so that ye cannot do the things that ye would. But if ye be led of the Spirit, ye are not under the law.*

Now the works of the flesh are manifest, which are these; Adultery, fornication, uncleanness, lasciviousness, Idolatry, witchcraft, hatred, variance, emulations, wrath, strife, seditions, heresies, Envyings, murders, drunkenness, revellings, and such like: of the which I tell you before, as I have also told you in time past, that they which do such things shall not inherit the kingdom of God. But the fruit of the Spirit is love, joy, peace, longsuffering, gentleness, goodness, faith, Meekness, temperance: against such there is no law. And they that are Christ's have crucified the flesh with the affections and lusts."

If Jesus Christ needed to die to redeem you from sin, then you also need to die to your fleshly desires in order to stay redeemed. You cannot continue to gratify all your carnal inclinations all in the name of liberty or being under grace. Your flesh is the devil's easiest access into your life because it is the part of you that doesn't get saved automatically unlike your spirit that got recreated immediately at conversion.

Your flesh doesn't respect your anointing, church title, or the length of time you spend in church services; it only respects your conscious efforts geared towards its mortification (death) through serious watching and praying, fasting, quality time spent in the Word of God and serious discipline (all through the help of the Holy Spirit).

There is another thing you need to know about

your flesh (carnal nature); it doesn't die on its own, it has to be crucified (subjected to painful death). And there is no one to do this for you, you are the one to carry out its execution because if you don't kill it, it has the capacity to kill you physically and even eternally. That's why Apostle Paul said in 1 Corinthians 9:27 NLT: *'I discipline my body like an athlete, training it to do what it should. Otherwise, I fear that after preaching to others I myself might be disqualified.'*

And he went further to say in Galatians 2:20 KJV: *'I am crucified with Christ: nevertheless I live; yet not I, but Christ liveth in me: and the life which I now live in the flesh I live by the faith of the Son of God, who loved me, and gave himself for me.'*

To tolerate your flesh or to constantly yield to its desires (carnality) is like drinking poison and hoping it won't do you any harm. That's simply suicidal!

Deal with your flesh before it deals with you; that's the devil living with you!

ANTHONY ADEFARAKAN

Principle #5

Becoming a Worthy Representative

Ephesians 4:1 GNT says *"I urge you, then--I who am a prisoner because I serve the Lord: live a life that measures up to the standard God set when he called you."*

The best favour God can enjoy from you as a believer is your worthy representation of His Kingdom everywhere you go. He is a Spirit, and the only way people can have an idea of Who He really is, is by looking at His followers – their ways of life, their habits, their decisions, their appearances, their choices of words, their reactions to opposing views and their general demeanour.

Nothing attracts disgrace to God more than any of His children (or followers) dragging His Holy Name in the mud through their actions or behaviour. That's one pain the Lord had when David decided to act in a way that wasn't worthy of a representative of the Most High. Despite being God's chosen king, he yielded to his carnal inclinations by having an unholy affair with Bathsheba, and even killed her husband in order to cover up his sinful deed. Those actions brought disgrace to God's Name and He expressed His displeasure to David through the message He gave prophet Nathan to deliver to him. According to 2 Samuel 12:1-12, the Lord used the prophet to pronounce judgment on David for committing such wickedness. And if you read verses 13-15 in King James Version, you would notice that prophet Nathan mentioned that David's sin gave God's enemies the opportunity to blaspheme (to speak reproachfully against His Holy Name): *'And David said unto Nathan, I have sinned against the LORD. And Nathan said unto David, The LORD also hath put away thy sin; thou shalt not die. Howbeit, because by this deed thou hast given great occasion to the ene-*

mies of the LORD to blaspheme, the child also that is born unto thee shall surely die. And Nathan departed unto his house. And the LORD struck the child that Uriah's wife bare unto David, and it was very sick.'

It is possible people were already saying things like: 'look at God's own chosen king committing adultery and even covering it up with murder; how could God call such a person His chosen? What kind of God is that?' People must have questioned God's choice of David as king because of his unbecoming behaviour.

Before you make the decision to take certain actions or to be involved in certain activities, take a moment to ask yourself if the outcome of such actions or activities would bring glory to God's Name or drag it in the mud. Will God be honoured or people will have the opportunity to say 'how could God call this person His own child?' The moment you surrender your life to Jesus Christ, you become branded for God and you are easily recognized and noticed everywhere you go because you are simply His representative here on earth. Carry that consciousness with you everywhere you go so you don't get carried away and start behaving like someone who doesn't have a relationship with God.

Now that your attention has been drawn to this matter, please live in such a way that God will not be ashamed of calling you His Own. God's grace is sufficient for you in Jesus' Name.

Principle #6

Escaping Spiritual Misery

Deuteronomy 29:29 NKJV says *"The secret things belong to the LORD our God, but those things which are revealed belong to us and to our children forever, that we may do all the words of this law."*

And 2 Timothy 3:7 KJV says *"Ever learning, and never able to come to the knowledge of the truth."*

Continuous discovery of scriptural truths without corresponding applications is a gateway to perpetual spiritual misery.

Our opening text says the secret things belong to God but the ones He has chosen to reveal belong to us and our children so we can apply them. With knowledge comes responsibility; you are held accountable for the knowledge at your disposal.

The Word of God is not just to be read, studied, or meditated on; it is also meant to be applied. What is the essence of having knowledge and not using it? That puts you in the same category as someone who doesn't know at all.

For instance, you have seen in the scriptures that Jesus took away your infirmity and that by His stripes you were healed, but you still go around with sicknesses in your body without doing anything about it. You don't exercise your faith for healing, and you don't confess what the Word of God says about your health, so you remain sick. Now, what is the difference between you and someone who doesn't even know one thing the Word of God has said about healing? You both will suffer the same fate.

14 SCRIPTURAL PRINCIPLES FOR DAILY LIVING
VOL. 4

James 1:22-25 NLT says *'But don't just listen to God's word. You must do what it says. Otherwise, you are only fooling yourselves. For if you listen to the word and don't obey, it is like glancing at your face in a mirror. You see yourself, walk away, and forget what you look like. But if you look carefully into the perfect law that sets you free, and if you do what it says and don't forget what you heard, then God will bless you for doing it.'*

Did you see that? The blessing is not in mere hearing or reading, the blessing is in the doing. So when it comes to the Word of God, the rule is: ***'Don't just see it, also do it!'***

Principle #7

Inexplicable Grace

1 Corinthians 15:9-10 NIV says *"I am the least of the apostles and do not even deserve to be called an apostle, because I persecuted the church of God. But by the grace of God I am what I am, and his grace to me was not without effect. No, I worked harder than all of them—yet not I, but the grace of God that was with me."*

Take note of the following scriptural verses:

Acts 13:9-11 NIV: *'Then Saul, who was also called Paul, filled with the Holy Spirit, looked straight at Elymas and said, "You are a child of the devil and an enemy of everything that is right! You are full of all kinds of deceit and trickery. Will you never stop perverting the right ways of the Lord? Now the hand of the Lord is against you. You are going to be blind for a time, not even able to see the light of the sun."*

Immediately mist and darkness came over him, and he groped about, seeking someone to lead him by the hand.'

Acts 14:8-10 NIV: *'In Lystra there sat a man who was lame. He had been that way from birth and had never walked. He listened to Paul as he was speaking. Paul looked directly at him, saw that he had faith to be healed and called out, "Stand up on your feet!" At that, the man jumped up and began to walk.'*

Acts 16:16-18 NIV: *'Once when we were going to the place of prayer, we were met by a female slave who had a spirit by which she predicted the future. She earned a great deal of money for her owners by fortune-telling. She followed Paul and the rest of us, shouting, "These men are servants of the Most High God, who are telling you the way to be saved." She kept this up for many days. Finally Paul became so annoyed that he turned around and said to the spirit, "In the name of Jesus Christ I command you to come out of her!" At that moment the spirit left her.'*

Acts 19:11-12 NIV: *'God did extraordinary miracles through Paul, so that even handkerchiefs and aprons that had touched him were taken to the sick, and their illnesses were cured and the evil spirits left them.'*

Acts 20:7-12 NIV: *'On the first day of the week we came together to break bread. Paul spoke to the people and, because he intended to leave the next day, kept on talking until midnight. There were many lamps in the upstairs room where we were meeting. Seated in a window was a young man named Eutychus, who was sinking into a deep sleep as Paul talked on and on. When he was sound asleep, he fell to the ground from the third story and was picked up dead. Paul went down, threw himself on the young man and put his arms around him. "Don't be alarmed," he said. "He's alive!" Then he went upstairs again and broke bread and ate. After talking until daylight, he left. The people took the young man home alive and were greatly comforted.'*

Acts 28:3-6 NIV: *'Paul gathered a pile of brushwood and, as he put it on the fire, a viper, driven out by the heat, fastened itself on his hand. When the islanders saw the snake hanging from his hand, they said to each other, "This man must be a murderer; for though he escaped from the sea, the goddess Justice has not allowed him to live." But Paul shook the snake off into the fire and suffered no ill effects. The people expected him to swell up or suddenly fall dead; but after waiting a long time and seeing nothing unusual happen to him, they changed their minds and said he was a god.'*

Acts 28:7-9 NIV: *'There was an estate nearby that belonged to Publius, the chief official of the island. He welcomed us to his home and showed us generous hospitality for three days. His father was sick in bed, suffering from fever and dysentery. Paul went in to see him and, after prayer, placed his hands on him and healed him. When this had happened, the rest of the sick on the island came and were cured.'*

Each of those verses referred to miracles performed by Apostle Paul during his time. God did the most unusual things through him.

Now, which Paul are we talking about? He's the same one previously known as Saul, who violently persecuted the Church and sought every way to destroy those who believed in Jesus.

But when grace located him on the road to Damascus, he became so transformed that he wasn't only preaching the same gospel he initially sought to destroy but was also performing signs and wonders (by the power of the Lord) to prove that Jesus is the Way. That was raw inexplicable grace.

If your success story can be explained by man, then it is probably man-made. But when the happenings in your life transcend human explanations, then you are beginning to understand the word 'GRACE'. Receive grace for supernatural advancement this season in the Name of Jesus.

Principle #8

Jesus' Love Language

John 14:15 KJV says *"If ye love me, keep my commandments."*

Jesus never said 'if you love me, say so', neither did he say 'if you love me, go to church and don't miss any of the services'. Rather, He said *'If you love me, keep my commandments'* – that is, do whatever I ask you to do.

Clarke's Commentary on this verse of the Bible reads: 'If ye love me, keep my commandments - Do not be afflicted at the thought of my being separated from you: the most solid proof ye can give of your attachment to and affection for me is to keep my commandments. This I shall receive as a greater proof of your affection than your tears.'

According to this Bible commentary, Jesus was telling His disciples that He feels more loved by their obedience than by their tears.

You know, in the natural, when you love someone you are usually emotionally attached to the person. You express words of affection and admiration when talking to them. You act in such a way that everyone looking will know you are fond of that person. But that is not the way the Lord feels loved. He doesn't feel loved by your emotional attachment and expressions, words of affection, and the likes. What makes Him feel so loved is your obedience to His commands (and the length you are willing to go in carrying them out). When you begin to treasure God's commands more than your necessary food like Job said in Job 23:12 NKJV - *'I have not departed from the commandment of His lips; I have treasured the words of His mouth More than my necessary food'* – then, you are beginning to understand how to speak the Lord's love language.

When obeying God is no longer a matter of whether it is convenient, you are getting to understand how He wants to be loved.

And just in case you don't remember, the first and the most important commandment is found in Matthew 22:37-38 BSB: *Jesus declared, 'Love the Lord your God with all your heart and with all your soul and with all your mind.' This is the first and greatest commandment.'*

Now, if the way the Lord wants to be loved is by keeping His commandments, it then follows that the first and the greatest commandment according to Jesus actually implies *'obey the Lord your God with all your heart and with all your soul and with all your mind.'* Little wonder the blessings of obedience are so great and attractive (Deuteronomy 28:1-14).

Jesus demonstrated His love for His Father by

doing everything He told Him to do, even when it meant dying a shameful death on the cross in full public view. He never failed God.

At a point, the weight was too much on Him and He wanted to opt-out of the plan; but then He remembered He had to please His Father, so He asked that the will of God be done and not His own will (Matthew 26:26-44). That's why in response to His total submission, the Almighty God exalted Him and gave Him a Name that is above every other name in Heaven, on earth, and beneath the earth, that at the mention of His Name, every knee should bow (Philippians 2:5-11).

Nothing pleases the Lord more than your obedience to His commands (whether it makes sense to you or not). 1 Samuel 15:22 GNT says '...*Which does the LORD prefer: obedience or offerings and sacrifices? It is better to obey him than to sacrifice the best sheep to him.*'

So, do you really love Jesus? Then, keep His

commandments. That's what makes Him feel loved.

Principle #9

Invest – Don't Spend

Proverbs 11:24-25 NKJV says *"There is one who scatters, yet increases more; And there is one who withholds more than is right, But it leads to poverty. The generous soul will be made rich, And he who waters will also be watered himself."*

Someone once said 'what you spend on yourself dies, but what you invest in others lives on'. That is why the Bible says *"...it is more blessed to give than to receive"* (Acts 20:35).

1 Samuel 22:1-2 NIV says *'David left Gath and escaped to the cave of Adullam. When his brothers and his father's household heard about it, they went down to him there. All those who were in distress or in debt or discontented gathered around him, and*

he became their commander. About four hundred men were with him.'

Take note of the conditions of these men who came to David – distressed, indebted, and discontented. They obviously weren't doing well in life.

Now, David did not judge them, rather he accepted them the way they were and invested in them until they became mighty men of valour. He taught them battle skills, sword techniques among other specialized training needed to succeed in battles. He poured out himself into them until they became giant killers like himself. Look at 2 Samuel 23:8-39 to see what those distressed men became as a result of David's investment in them. One of them lifted up his spear and killed 800 at one time; another one killed 300 in a single battle, while yet another one went down into a pit during the time of snow and killed a lion there. They all carried out great and wonderful acts because David invested in them and his God was also with them.

Nothing immortalizes a man better than investing in others. You simply live on even after death because of your indelible legacies.

Jesus spent years training and developing His disciples, and after He left, those disciples became world changers (in spite of the fact that some of them were illiterates). Spend time with your family; invest in your children; invest in your employees; as a Pastor, invest in your members until they are able to do what you do. Don't just live for yourself. Instead of buying that second car you really don't need, why not invest the money into providing food and education for the orphans or underprivileged ones in your neighbourhood? Did you know your investment into such lives may produce Presidents of nations in the future? You never can tell how great the returns on such investments will be.

Share your life with others, that's how to keep living after death. May the Lord bless your heart as you take action in this direction in Jesus' Name.

Principle #10

Stop Tolerating It

Acts 16:16-18 KJV says *"And it came to pass, as we went to prayer, a certain damsel possessed with a spirit of divination met us, which brought her masters much gain by soothsaying: The same followed Paul and us, and cried, saying, These men are the servants of the most high God, which shew unto us the way of salvation. And this did she many days. But Paul, being grieved, turned and said to the spirit, I command thee in the name of Jesus Christ to come out of her. And he came out the same hour."*

And James 4:7 GNT says *"So then, submit yourselves to God. Resist the Devil, and he will run away from you."*

Are you born again? If yes, please stop tolerating any experience you know can't be traced to Jesus Christ. Remember, He is the Vine, and *'ye are the branches'* (John 15:1-5). Therefore if Jesus (the Vine) can't accommodate it, then 'ye' as the branch have no business tolerating it.

Look at our opening text; a demon-possessed girl had been following and disturbing Apostle Paul and his team for many days until Paul got irritated and cast the spirit out of the girl.

Now, why did that girl disturb them for many days? Because they were willing to tolerate her disturbance. However, the day Paul got fed up and couldn't take it any longer, he did something about it and the matter ended right there.

Whatever you are willing to tolerate has automatically been given the permission to persist. Demons for instance don't just go away because they have been in a place long enough or simply because you are a very nice person and you don't like disturbing anybody. If they must leave, they will have to be told to leave. They must be cast out or else they remain where they are.

In Mark 5:1-20, a mad man who was housing a legion of demons (about 6,000) met Jesus and worshipped Him. Those demons saw Jesus and recognized Him, but they didn't leave the man just because they saw Jesus. It was only when Jesus commanded them to leave his body that they actually left. That mad man worshipped Jesus (even in his madness) because he knew only Jesus could set him free. You can be in church and still be obsessed, depressed, possessed, or even oppressed. Being in church won't set you free; those forces have to be told to leave your life before your freedom can manifest.

Stop tolerating sin, evil thoughts, carnal desires, unholy relationships, sicknesses, bad habits, poverty, demonic influences, and the likes. If you don't like them, then do something about them. The Bible says, provided you have submitted your life to God, you can resist the devil (tell him to stop) and he will flee from you.

Don't tolerate that unfavorable condition for one more day. Your deliverance is here now in Jesus' Name.

Principle #11

Nothing Can Separate You

Romans 8:35-39 KJV *"Who shall separate us from the love of Christ? shall tribulation, or distress, or persecution, or famine, or nakedness, or peril, or sword?*

As it is written, For thy sake we are killed all the day long; we are accounted as sheep for the slaughter. Nay, in all these things we are more than conquerors through him that loved us. For I am persuaded, that neither death, nor life, nor angels, nor principalities, nor powers, nor things present, nor things to come, Nor height, nor depth, nor any other creature, shall be able to separate us from the love of God, which is in Christ Jesus our Lord."

The love God has for all His children is constant. You can't do anything to earn more and there's equally nothing you can do to make Him love you less. His love is not based on your performance or dedication; it is wholly based on Who He is – 1 John 4:8 says God is love.

Romans 5:8 NASB says *"...God demonstrates His own love toward us, in that while we were yet sinners, Christ died for us.'*

And John 15:13 NKJV says *'Greater love has no one than this, than to lay down one's life for his friends.'* Did you know that it is the love the Lord has for you that made Him undergo the agony of crucifixion at Calvary? If He could do that when you were still living in sin, what makes you think He doesn't love you again (more so now that you have known His Name)?

Nothing can separate you from the love of God which is in Christ Jesus our Lord. And all He wants from you is to love Him back (just as He has loved you).

Get this straight today; Jesus still loves you as He did when He took your place at Calvary. And nothing can separate you from that love. Please kindly be reassured, and live your life in alignment with that reality going forward.

Principle #12

Repent

Acts 3:19 NKJV says *"Repent therefore and be converted, that your sins may be blotted out, so that times of refreshing may come from the presence of the Lord,"*

The message of repentance is still relevant today because sin is still in the world. Not hearing it from the pulpit every Sunday doesn't mean you can continue sinning.

What does repentance actually mean? According to Wikipedia, repentance is the activity of reviewing one's actions and feeling contrition or regret for past wrongs, which is accompanied by commitment to and actual actions that show and prove a change for the better.

From this description, it means repentance has to do with a change of direction or a change of way; and there must be actions and commitment to prove that the change (for the better) has occurred.

For instance, if you are a fornicator with multiple sex partners; you can't claim you have repented if you only reduced your sin partners to one or two. To prove that you have repented, there shouldn't be any sin partner left in your life. 2 Corinthians 5:17 says if you are in Christ, you are a new creature, old things have passed away behold all things have become new. To become new, the old must be completely gone (not reduced).

What is that thing in your life that you know God is not happy with? What habit or behaviour do you indulge in that you know the Word of God expressly condemns? Repent. Stop doing it so you can avoid the wrath of God and consequently experience His time of refreshing.

John the Baptist speaking in Luke 3:8 NLT said *'Prove by the way you live that you have repented of your sins and turned to God. Don't just say to each other, 'We're safe, for we are descendants of Abraham.' That means nothing, for I tell you, God can create children of Abraham from these very stones.'*

The main theme of the message Jesus Christ preached during His earthly ministry was: *'Repent, for the Kingdom of God is at hand'* - (Matthew 4:17).

If you really belong to Jesus, you should do what He preached. Repent!

Principle #13

He Has All The Answers

1 Corinthians 1:24 NKJV says *"But to those called by God to salvation, both Jews and Gentiles, Christ is the power of God and the wisdom of God."*

And Proverbs 8:12-36 ERV says *"I am Wisdom. I live with Good Judgment. I am at home with Knowledge and Planning.*

To respect the Lord means to hate evil. I hate pride and boasting, evil lives and hurtful words. I have good advice and common sense to offer. I have understanding and power.

With my help kings rule, and governors make good laws. With my help leaders govern, and important officials make good decisions.

I love those who love me, and those who look for me will find me. With me there are riches and honor. I have lasting wealth to give to you.

What I give is better than fine gold. What I produce is better than pure silver.
I lead people the right way—along the paths of justice.

I give riches to those who love me, and I fill their houses with treasures. "The Lord made me in the beginning, long before he did anything else.

I was formed a long time ago, before the world was made.
I was born before there was an ocean, before the springs began to flow.

I was born before the mountains and hills were set into place, before the earth and fields were made, before the dust of this world was formed.

I was there when he set up the skies, when he drew a circle in the ocean to make a place for the land. I was there when he put the clouds in the sky and made the deep springs flow.

I was there when he set the limits on the sea to make it stop where he said. I was there when he laid the foundations of the earth. I grew up as a child by his side, laughing and playing all the time. I played in the world he made and enjoyed the people he put there.

"Now, children, listen to me. If you follow my ways, you will be happy too. Listen to my teaching and be wise; don't ignore what I say. Whoever waits at my door and listens for me will be blessed. Those who find me find life, and the Lord will reward them. But those who do not find me put their lives in danger. Whoever hates me loves death.""

What you have just read is what I call 'Wisdom's Profile". That's everything you can get from Wisdom – knowledge, insight, understanding, answers to deep questions, good and sound judgment, keys to riches, life, etc.

And according to our opening text, Jesus is both the Power of God and the Wisdom of God. So, you can safely refer to "Wisdom's Profile" as "Jesus' Profile". All you can get from Wisdom you can get from Jesus because He is the Wisdom of God Personified.

What does that mean? It means He has all the answers to life's questions (including the ones that have been bothering you). There is nothing God does not know because He is the Source of all knowledge. Therefore, if you have a relationship with Jesus (God's Knowledge Centre), you can never lack answers to your questions.

So, what question or matter has been bothering your mind? What has been causing confusion in your thoughts? Jesus is the answer to all questions in life. Why not go ahead and ask Him? – Matthew 7:7-8.

Principle #14

Walking in the Spirit

Galatians 5:16-25 KJV says *"This I say then, Walk in the Spirit, and ye shall not fulfil the lust of the flesh. For the flesh lusteth against the Spirit, and the Spirit against the flesh: and these are contrary the one to the other: so that ye cannot do the things that ye would. But if ye be led of the Spirit, ye are not under the law.*

Now the works of the flesh are manifest, which are these; Adultery, fornication, uncleanness, lasciviousness, Idolatry, witchcraft, hatred, variance, emulations, wrath, strife, seditions, heresies, Envyings, murders, drunkenness, revellings, and such like: of the which I tell you before, as I have also told you in time past, that they which do such things shall not inherit the kingdom of God. But the fruit of the Spirit is love, joy, peace, longsuffering, gentleness, goodness, faith, Meekness, temperance: against such there is no law. And they that are Christ's have crucified the flesh with the affections and lusts.

If we live in the Spirit, let us also walk in the Spirit."

Walking in the Spirit is the hallmark of victory over sin. It is the surest way to subduing the flesh and its lustful desires.

What then does 'walking in the Spirit' mean? It means living above the desires of the flesh; not yielding to carnal inclinations despite the pressure to do so. And there is only one way to accomplish this (after surrendering your life to Jesus Christ of course); it is by living a Word-governed life. That is, to walk in the Spirit actually means to live by the Word of God. Jesus speaking in John 6:63 NKJV said *'It is the Spirit who gives life; the flesh profits nothing. The words that I speak to you are spirit, and they are life'*. And David also said in Psalm

119:11 that hiding God's word in one's heart can prevent one from sinning.

So, are you finding it difficult to resist temptations to sin despite your fasting, prayers, and New Year resolutions? Struggle no more; the solution is to begin walking in the Spirit. Get into the Word of God and store its truths in your heart through conscious and disciplined meditation. You will soon discover how easy the Holy Spirit uses those truths stored in your heart to help you overcome temptations of every kind. May the grace to live above sin rest upon you in Jesus' Name.

Conclusion

So far, the Lord has revealed some biblical principles to us. The purpose is not just to know, document, or preach them, rather they were revealed so that we can walk in them.

According to John 8:32, only the truth that is known sets free. So, go through these principles one by one and determine to build your Christian walk around them for a life of Kingdom impact here on earth.

Jesus said in John 13:17(NLT) - *"You know these things- now do them! That is the path of blessing."*

May the Lord release upon you and your entire household the grace to walk worthy of His calling upon your lives in Jesus' Name!

WHY YOU REALLY NEED JESUS!

You might have heard a lot of Preachers talk about the importance of surrendering one's life to Jesus and even the dangers of not doing so at one time or the other without you being really moved. But with these three (3) important reasons highlighted below, I strongly believe you will not need another sermon before deciding to yield to His saving grace regardless of your religious beliefs.

1. **You have an Enemy to overcome:** There is an adversary who is all out to steal from you, kill you and destroy you regardless of your level of education, moral uprightness, societal influence, or even religious beliefs. He is Devil by name (John 10:10, 1 Peter 5: 8), and he doesn't release any of

his captives until he completely destroys their souls in hell. The ONLY One Who can deliver you from his manipulations and also save your soul from him is Jesus Christ.

2. **You have an Appointment to keep:** Being alive and reading this implies you have a very important and inevitable appointment to keep. It is an appointment with death (Hebrews 9:27). Death is the sure end of all mortals (of which you are part), and to enable you prepare for this appointment without fear of eternal damnation, you need Jesus. He is the ONLY One Who has power over death (Revelation 1:18).

3. **You have a Judge to face:** Upon departure from this earth, you will have to stand before a judgment throne to render an account of your earthly life (Hebrews 9:27, Romans 14:12). The outcome of this judgment is what will determine your eternal abode which will either be Heaven

or the Lake of fire. Interestingly, the Judge Who will preside over your case and also decide where you will spend your eternity is Jesus (John 5:21-30, 2 Timothy 4:1). I perceive you are thinking "is God not our Judge? Why Jesus?' Well, you are not wrong. But God the Father Himself is the One Who handed over all the judgment to His Son, Jesus Christ. Read verse 22 of that John chapter 5. So Jesus is the ONLY One Who has the power to either judge you guilty or guiltless in eternity.

Now that you know these, the wisest thing you can do for yourself is to quickly establish a relationship with Jesus, since you don't even know how close your appointment with death is. To do this, say this prayer aloud:

"Lord Jesus, I am a sinner and I cannot help myself. Wash me in your precious blood and make me a new creature. I open the door of my heart to you today, come into my life and become my Lord and Savior. Grant me the grace

to overcome the devil, prepare me for eternity and help me to escape the judgment reserved for sinners. Thank You Jesus for saving me. Amen."

Congratulations! You are now SAVED. Go and sin no more.

To learn more about your new relationship with Jesus, kindly send an Email to info@gloem.org or emancipation4souls@yahoo.com, we will send you a material that will help you. You can also call, text, or send a WhatsApp message to +1 587 9735910 or +1 587 9695910 for further assistance.

And to learn more about God, His Word, and His plans for your life, kindly visit our Facebook page [***https://www.facebook.com/gloem.org***] for daily meditation in the Word of God (all year round) and our Blog page [***https://gloem.org/myblog***] for life-transforming publications.

You are also invited to listen to Freedom Podcast: The Official Weekly Podcast of Global Emancipation Ministries – Calgary via https://anchor.fm/gloem

All these great resources capable of developing your spiritual stamina will help you become an overcomer in life regardless of what comes your way.

PRAYER POINTS

1. Father, thank You for opening my eyes to the truths contained in this book.
2. Father, please cause every experience in my life to work together for my good.
3. I cancel everything contrary to my spiritual advancement in Jesus' Name.
4. God of all possibilities, please cause my grass to become green again.
5. From today, the fulfillment of my expectations shall no longer be delayed in Jesus' Name.
6. Father, beginning from now, please release upon me and my household the ability to walk with you faithfully in the Name of Jesus.
7. Father, I thank You for answering all my

prayers. Glory be to Your Holy Name. Hallelujah!

BECOME A FINANCIAL PARTNER WITH JESUS

At *Global Emancipation Ministries - Calgary*, our mandate is *to liberate men through the knowledge of the Truth* and our mission statement is *creating channels through which men can encounter the Truth - [Isaiah 61:1-3; John 8:32, 36; I Thessalonians 5:24].*

Our Ministerial Activities include Rural and Urban Evangelical Outreaches, Prison Evangelism, Hospital Ministrations, Mobilization for Missions Support, Teaching of the undiluted Word of God, Scripture-Based Seminars, Discipleship, Training of Field Missionaries and Empowerment of underprivileged ones among other Field Ministerial Tasks.

If you sense the Lord is calling you to reach out to the lost by engaging in any of these activities or by assisting those involved with your resources, please feel free to join us. Let us come together as we take the Gospel of our Lord Jesus Christ to the hurting and forgotten ones. [Mark 16:15-20].

Please join us in these kingdom projects by making your weekly, monthly, quarterly, or annual donations to Global Emancipation Ministries – Calgary.

You can visit the "GIVE" section on our website, www.gloem.org, to learn about the ways to give.

For acknowledgment, please advise your donations to us by email: info@gloem.org or emancipation4souls@yahoo.com, and kindly include your details i.e. name, address, email, and location. Alternatively, you can simply call +1 587 9735910 to do the same.

You can also volunteer your gifts and talents

in the service of the Lord through our ministerial platforms regardless of your location. To get information on how to go about this, please visit www.gloem.org and contact us via email: info@gloem.org or emancipation4souls@yahoo.com.

God bless you.

About the Author

By the special grace of God, **Anthony O. Adefarakan** is the privileged President of **Global Emancipation Ministries - Calgary (GLOEM)** with headquarters in Canada, North America, and **Emancipating Truth Ministry International (ETMI)** with headquarters in Nigeria, West Africa.

The Lord called him into the field ministry in February 2008 with the mandate to liberate men through the knowledge of the Truth, and by December 2012 he was ordained and commissioned as the Pioneer Pastor – in – Charge of The Redeemed Christian Church of God, Revelation Parish, Shalom Area under Delta Province III, Nigeria where he served until 1st February 2015 when he officially handed over to a new Pastor in order to focus on his field ministry to which the Lord had earlier called him and for which the authority of the church had already prayed and released him to undertake.

On 29th September 2013, he was awarded a Post Graduate Diploma in Tent – Making Mission from the Redeemed Christian School of Missions, Nigeria (RECSOM, Asaba Campus) where he also had the privilege to train Pastors and Missionaries as a lecturer in 2017.

Since the commissioning of his field ministry in 2015 he has had the opportunity to lead his ministry officers to field ministrations in different Prisons, Hospitals, Orphanages, Rural communities, Camp settlements, Markets, Local churches among other places with great successes on all occasions – such as the salvation of sinners, healing of the sick, financial empowerment of mission churches, provision of relief materials to the poor, provision of medical services to the underprivileged, baptism in the Holy Ghost, deliverance from demonic oppression, the release of inmates just to mention a few - all to the glory of God Who alone is the Doer.

He is the author of other best-selling titles such as *The Law of Kinds, Learning From the Ants, The Immutability of God's Counsel, Surely there is an End, Life Applicable lessons from the Book of Ruth, One thing is Needful Weekly Devotional Guide, Life Applicable Revelations from God's Word* (Volumes 1 and 2) among others.

He is blissfully married to Ifeoluwa A. Adefarakan and their marriage is fruitful to the glory of God.

Jesus is his Message, Freedom is the Outcome! Isaiah 61:1-3.

www.ingramcontent.com/pod-product-compliance
Lightning Source LLC
Chambersburg PA
CBHW022231080526
44577CB00005B/145